Christopher King

Aus der Reihe: e-fellows.net stipendiaten-wissen

e-fellows.net (Hrsg.)

Band 810

Brzezinski and Maddow on American Power

Book Review

GRIN Verlag

Bibliografische Information der Deutschen Nationalbibliothek:

Die Deutsche Bibliothek verzeichnet diese Publikation in der Deutschen National-
bibliografie; detaillierte bibliografische Daten sind im Internet über http://dnb.d-
nb.de/ abrufbar.

Imprint:

Copyright © 2012 GRIN Verlag GmbH
Druck und Bindung: Books on Demand GmbH, Norderstedt Germany
ISBN: 978-3-656-51073-4

This book at GRIN:

http://www.grin.com/en/e-book/262774/brzezinski-and-maddow-on-american-
power

GRIN - Your knowledge has value

Der GRIN Verlag publiziert seit 1998 wissenschaftliche Arbeiten von Studenten, Hochschullehrern und anderen Akademikern als eBook und gedrucktes Buch. Die Verlagswebsite www.grin.com ist die ideale Plattform zur Veröffentlichung von Hausarbeiten, Abschlussarbeiten, wissenschaftlichen Aufsätzen, Dissertationen und Fachbüchern.

Visit us on the internet:

http://www.grin.com/

http://www.facebook.com/grincom

http://www.twitter.com/grin_com

Indiana University

College of Arts & Sciences

Department of Political Science

Fall 2012

POLS-Y360: United States Foreign Policy

Book Review

Zbigniew Brzezinski (2012): Strategic Vision. America and the Crisis of Global Power

Rachel Maddow (2012): Drift. The unmooring of American military power

Christopher King

International Exchange Student in the Undergraduate Program

Table of Content

1. Introduction

The future of America's position in the world is a hotly debated topic and this paper will review two books on American power and military capability. Zbigniew Brzezinski observes in "Strategic Vision" that a shift in world power occurs and so has to change the strategy of the USA. He assesses different liabilities and assets that need to be considered in dealing with these changes. Rachel Maddow however has a different emphasis in "Drift" and is concerned about the development of perpetual American war and the responsible but unchecked executive branch. In the following will be argued that while other nations may rise, the USA can still sustain its position of power, if it considers the research of Brzezinski and Maddow to be of relevance. Reforms at home and readiness to transition into a world shared with nations that rise or come back to their old greatness will be needed to use America's power and resources in the future more wisely. America will continue to be a world power if it avoids mistakes it makes right now at home and embraces the new realities of the world.

2. Brzezinski and Maddow on American Power

There is a lot of fuss right now about the "American decline". In a 2011 poll 39% of Americans saw their country in "permanent decline" (cf. Montopoli 2011), so when writing about the future of American power one needs first to make things clear about the controversial decline theme. While the dominant anxious pattern of decline is dominating the news, scholars tend to estimate the situation differently. The executive summary of the Global Trends report predicts America to be a less dominant power by 2025 (cf. Atlantic Council 2008).

2.1 Brzezinski

For Brzezinski, American decline is a possible scenario if the right political steps won't be taken, but not yet a political reality (cf. Brzezinski 2012: 72ff.). Joseph S. Nye argues instead that the debate itself is exaggerated and the term decline overinflated, because there are certain changes to be observed but they don't necessarily have to lead to a decline as America will comparatively remain powerful (cf. Nye 2012). However Fareed Zakaria says that a "relative decline" will occur, because he sees like Brzezinski a global power shift happening and terms it, the now popular quoted, "the rise of the rest" (Zakaria 2008a). Nye concludes his essay on the future of American power with a call for a U.S. strategy that uses hard- and soft-power assets (cf. Nye 2010: 12); can Brzezinski's "Strategic Vision" offer that?

Brzezinski seeks to present a strategic vision for the USA that copes with the redistribution of global power to prevent U.S. decline. An essential precondition of this outlook is that America solves its domestic issues and fixes its liabilities at home (cf. Brzezinski 2012: 46ff.). It would be capable to do so, because it has solid assets and some of the current problems are self-made and could be stopped or solved (cf. Brzezinski 2012: 72ff.). Nye and Zakaria join Brzezinski in his diagnosis of American diseases in its political system. Nye said already in 2002 that American power will continue but only if used wisely (cf. Nye 2002: 546). From today's perspective, this sounds almost like a foreshadowing of the wrong Iraq war. Brzezinski presumably would more than agree to that as he argues that America can just sustain its power if it stops making Foreign Policy mistakes like the war in Iraq. Similar to Brzezinski, Zakaria sees the problem of non-functioning U.S. politics that delay or even prevent the coherent solving of policy challenges that are so vital for the future of American power. The empire of Britain declined back in history not because of political problems, but rather due to economic shortcomings. Zakaria uses this example and argues now, that America currently faces the reverse threat (cf. Zakaria 2008b: 40ff.).

2.2 Maddow

The book of Rachel Maddow is extremely relevant in that regard, because it relates well to the "Brzezinskian" overarching theme of American power and the problems accompanying it, as it offers an insightful new perspective on how the role of the military changed. Her main point in "Drift" is that the evolved almost unchecked, quasi sole presidential power on the use of force led to war-prone developments for the USA that drove the nation and its military off course. For Maddow, the future of America's position in the world will similar to Brzezinski rather depend on reforming America than looking anxious at rising nations. Her arguments are persuasive and she receives credits for her book from both sides of the political spectrum. Maddow takes a similar line as Brzezinski and is concerned about spending, she especially points out to failures in military spending (cf. Maddow 2012: 22ff.) and shows that the privatization and outsourcing of U.S. Foreign Policy was and will be harmful for America's position in the long term (cf. Maddow 2012: 166f.). Worse for her is that the American public nowadays isn't even aware of America's use of military power because of the extensive application of covert special operations and drone strikes (cf. Maddow 2012: 176f.). Stephen M. Walt sees that as a problem for America's position in the world as well, because an uninformed American public then won't understand why people from other countries are mad at America, which causes even more misunderstandings and stereotypes that could lead to potential clashes in the future (cf. Walt 2012).

2.3 Assessment

Following Brzezinski's vision the USA needs to work on enlarging the West to be able to sustain America's power by ensuring stability in the world, which would thereof consolidate its future position as well (cf. Brzezinski 2012: 102f.). I don't disagree with him on that but as a European myself I can't follow his perception of the European Union and stay skeptical of the feasibility of his enlargement model. Most important, I don't see any scenario in the future and even in the long term that Turkey could and will join the EU. And I don't consider either that in light of Europe's economic crisis any country will raise their defense spending and be capable of real commitments to NATO defense, as seen in Libya, so his strategy shouldn't be designed to be too dependent on a successful "enlargement of the west". But I highly sympathize with his approach to dedicate a big part of his book to domestic problems and the need to solve them because a suffering America at home won't be capable of sustaining its position and influence in the world.

So how is America positioned for the future? Brzezinski and Zakaria coincide in ambivalent assessments: American decline is not inevitable, its gems are its GDP per capita and favorable demographic numbers due to an inflow of educated immigrants, but America's non-functioning political system hinders solution-solving of domestic obstacles. Furthermore Zakaria makes an interesting point in saying that America forgot to learn from others, because it dominated the world for such a long time. But at this point in history it is crucial to learn, reform and adapt to the upcoming changes to stay competitive (cf. Zakaria 2008b: 38f.). It is overdue to bring in Maddow's analysis again at this point. It seems unimaginable that the U.S. could afford another overstretch like Afghanistan and Iraq in times of tight budget control. Boots on the ground will be avoided and covert operations and drone strikes preferred, but they aren't a sophisticated Foreign Policy strategy either to sustain leadership in a multi-polarized world. What Maddow really bothers is how the role of the military has been changed in America and how easy, or better how hard to oppose, it is to deploy Special Forces around the world without the American public being even slightly disturbed.

The outlook for America's future position in the world in light of the remarks of Brzezinski and Maddow is hard to assess, but there is not too much of a reason to be overly pessimistic at this point. There are some solid considerations why the prospects a for continued American power aren't too bad: It will remain to be the military and economic powerhouse in the world for a long time, America's presence and leadership is still wanted in regions like the Greater Middle East or Pacific Asia and China will presumably face some challenges like domestic unrest or extreme nationalism as well. Estimating the authors take on a prediction, I assume that for both Brzezinski and Maddow, American decline remains a real possibility if leaders fail to reform America and pursue the right strategy. A great deal of the certainty of America's future position in the world will be determined at home and severely depend on how the U.S. government manages the transition when it is not the sole superpower of the world anymore. That's admittedly a big if though, as the gridlocked Congress today is one deferrer of serious decision-making. Awareness and monitoring of the governmental role and functionality of Congress in the future is therefore highly recommended.

3. Conclusion

Both books offer convincing arguments about America's position in the future and are in their way an important addition to the study of American power. Brzezinski provides a solid vision in his realist analysis for a strategy that could enable the USA to address its problems at home and be present at the vital regions of the world. Although I'm skeptical of the feasibility of Turkey and Russia enlarging the West, I agree on that America needs to maintain the support for its allies as this is the key for well-functioning relationships that will prove to be ever more important. Maddow provides an essential understanding of the negative development of America's military role and her book adds probably the even bigger contribution to the field as it reveals unique insight into a long neglected development of the military and security branch of the United States.

America once managed to handle the hostile adversary Soviet Union in the Cold War. New challenges lie ahead, but if America gets on the right track as outlined by Brzezinski and Maddow, it will also be capable of staying powerful besides ascended other nations.

4. Bibliography

Atlantic Council (2008): Global Trends 2025: A Transformed World. Available online at
http://www.acus.org/publication/global-trends-2025-transformed-world, checked on
11/28/2012.

Brzezinski, Zbigniew (2012): Strategic Vision. America and the Crisis of Global Power. New
York: Basic Books.

Maddow, Rachel (2012): Drift. The unmooring of American military power. New York:
Crown.

Montopoli, Brian (2011): Poll: Many say economy is in permanent decline. With assistance of
Sarah Dutton, Jennifer de Pinto, Fred Backus, Anthony Salvanto. CBS News Polling
Unit. Available online at http://www.cbsnews.com/8301-503544_162-20075539-
503544.html, checked on 11/28/2012.

Nye, Joseph S., JR. (2002): Limits of American Power. In Political Science Quarterly 117 (4),
pp. 545–559.

Nye, Joseph S., JR. (2010): The Future of American Power. Dominance and Decline in
Perspective. In Foreign Affairs 89 (6), pp. 2–12.

Nye, Joseph S., JR. (2012): Declinist Pundits. America may not actually be declining, but
those predicting it are ascending. Foreign Policy. Available online at
http://www.foreignpolicy.com/articles/2012/10/08/declinist_pundits, checked on
11/28/2012.

Walt, Stephen M. (2012): Breaking the golden rule. Foreign Policy. Available online at
http://walt.foreignpolicy.com/posts/2012/06/01/breaking_the_golden_rule_0, checked
on 11/28/2012.

Zakaria, Fareed (2008a): The Rise of the Rest. Excerpt from "The Post-American World".
Available online at http://www.thedailybeast.com/newsweek/2008/05/03/the-rise-of-
the-rest.html, checked on 11/28/2012.

Zakaria, Fareed (2008b): The Future of American Power: How America Can Survive the Rise
of the Rest. In *Foreign Affairs* 87 (3), pp. 18–43.